The Pastureland
The Mountainside

Donna Riggs

The Pastureland and the Mountainside
by Donna Riggs
Copyright ©2025 Donna Riggs
ISBN 978-1-63360-296-0

For Worldwide Distribution Printed in the U.S.A.

Urban Press
P.O. Box 8881
Pittsburgh, PA 15221-0881 USA
412.646.2780
www.urbanpress.us

Introduction to
The Pastureland

Forty years ago, I went through an emotional breakdown and a long time of deep depression. Somehow I got ahold of a small paperback book entitled *God's Psychiatry* by Dr. Charles L. Allen, a pastor. His instructions were simple as he wrote about Psalm 23, the Ten Commandments, the Lord's Prayer, and the Beatitudes. As the book cover explained, "These prescriptions can be filled at the always-open courts of Heaven and are always renewable." They were intended to help the reader learn a new pattern of thinking about God and one's relationship to Him.

This is a compilation of journal entries I made while reading Psalm 23 as "prescribed" to *read* five times a day for a week (or more) then, and since, as I've re-read my original entries and added to them. Some reflect the very first time I read through the psalm as prescribed. Some reflect deeper insights into the verses from subsequent study. And some are even brand new as of this writing. It is, after all, the living Word!

As I reflected on each verse of the Psalm, I wrote it out along with the comments Dr. Allen had made. Then I wrote whatever came to me as I read the psalm each time each day. I've called this writing *The*

Pastureland for that is where the Shepherd leads us to feed and care for us. I had a surprising epiphany when reading over my journal this time. It will be explained in the section on verse 5a. I pray it will encourage and minister to you as you read.

Always Soli Deo Gloria!

God's Psychiatry, Charles L. Allen, ©1953 by Fleming H. Revell a division of Baker Book House Company, P.O. Box 6287, Grand Rapids, Michigan 49516-6287

God's Psychiatry Notes

Dr. Allen's method of reading the Psalm to form a new pattern of thinking about God brings healing to those who are anxious, depressed, and in need of a way of thinking that will breathe new life into their spirits. The bullet points after each verse are from Dr. Allen's introduction to Psalm 23. His directions were to read it five times each day for a week, thinking through each word and phrase and pausing for as long as the Holy Spirit arrests your attention. His points are followed by my reflections. And finally, space is left for you to write your own reflections. I pray you will be blessed to know the Shepherd of Psalm 23 in a much more personal way.

Psalm 23

Verse 1

"The Lord is my shepherd;
I shall not want."

- The sheep know the shepherd and have learned to trust him for everything they need.
- A calming statement of fact and assurance – we do not have to beg him for anything.

The first day I didn't get past trying to internalize and personalize "shepherd" and define "want." It was difficult for me to believe that the Lord could know everything I needed in the same way that a shepherd could understand the rather primitive needs of sheep. I found some Bible verses that helped me. In John 10:14 Jesus says of Himself, "I am the good shepherd, and know my sheep and my sheep know me." And Ezekiel 34:12 was a comfort to me. "As a shepherd looks after his scattered flock when he is with them, so will I look after my sheep. I will rescue them from all the places where they were scattered on a day of clouds and darkness." I certainly needed to be rescued and it was reassuring to know that if the Lord saw my need, He would care for me and I wouldn't lack or have to beg Him for anything.

The next day I spent on "the Lord" and surprisingly on "not." These days gave me a new understanding of what it means to have a professed relationship with *my* Shepherd and the assurance of His care. This led me to Philippians 4:19: "And my God will supply all your needs according to His riches in glory by Christ Jesus."

There was a day when I closed my eyes and envisioned Jesus before me with His right hand extended to me saying, "Follow me." I felt so loved and cared for. I felt anxiety slipping away. I felt blessed to think that my safety and salvation could bring glory to my Shepherd.

Your Reflections

Verse 2a

"He makes me to lie down in green pastures"

• Sheep walk as they graze and after about six hours, they are tired, overheated, and thirsty—but the shepherd knows they must not drink when they are full of undigested grass; he makes them rest in cool, shady spots.

I have felt that since my breakdown I have not been useful, even to my family, because of the anxiety. I have been confused that since coming to Christ I have felt more frightened and afraid to be with people than before. Today's revelation of this passage is that even though I feel I am in the midst of "green pastures" and should be doing something useful, the Shepherd has said, "Lie down, rest, and when it is time to do something, I will let you know." Relief. I will await my traveling orders.

The Shepherd wants me to know "my times are in Your [His] hands" (Psalm 31:15). Change does not happen by chance but is God's orchestrated plan for my life. In his commentary on the 23rd Psalm, Matthew Henry has written, "Let us not think it enough to pass through [the green pastures], but let us lie down in them, abide in them; this is my rest for ever. It is by this constancy of grace that the soul is fed."

This constancy of grace! What an amazing, assuring, heart-stirring thought.

Your Reflections

Verse 2b

"He leads me beside still waters"

- Sheep are afraid of swift currents because they are poor swimmers.
- Sheep will not drink from a moving stream.
- The shepherd understands their fears, so if still waters are not available the shepherd dams up an area from which they can drink from slowly moving pools – not from stagnant, bad-tasting water.
- God does not condemn us for weaknesses and fears – He doesn't force us, but ministers to our needs.

When He is ready, He will lead me to "drink" when this nourishing "meal" has been digested. He doesn't condemn me for my fears but will lead me to places I need not fear. He has created "still waters" within me by opening a canal to allow me passage from the turbulent, landlocked lake I used to be in to the River of Life which flows from Him. He has performed a bypass on my soul. All praise to Him!

Your Reflections

Verse 3a

"He restores my soul"

- Sheep go to the shepherd for special attention, petting, personal care.
- God revives life in us when we have lost our spiritual strength.

He has indeed performed a bypass around the debris of fear. I am delivered! I feel brand new! This level of grace may not be understood by an unbeliever, but to a believer the goodness of God toward them revives and satisfies their desperately hungering, thirsting soul. Consider the deer in Psalm 42, crashing through the underbrush in a desperate search for water. He will die if he does not find the water that will quench his parched tongue, throat, and lungs.

"As the deer pants for the water brooks,
So pants my soul for You, O God.
My soul thirsts for God, for the living God."
Psalm 42:1

Your Reflections

Verse 3b

"He leads me in the paths of righteousness for His name's sake"

- Sheep have no sense of direction and are easily lost – they also have poor eyesight and can step off of a precipice to injury or death.
- God walks with us and leads us into the right paths – all we have to do is follow.
- The Shepherd directs us to the paths that are best for our welfare and confirm His perfect will.

"My Shepherd, I feel You are leading me in a certain direction, but I'm not sure where. Come closer, Shepherd, so I can know Your will." Some days later I feel He wants me to write for His glory. As a confirmation, the pastor of my church asked me to write an article for the church newsletter defending a political candidate from a Christian point of view. I feel expectant and I wait for further orders.

The NIV Bible notes that this can be understood as the paths that conform to God's moral will. It says, "The prosperity of the Lord's servant brings honor to the Lord's Name." (Psalm 35:27) Prosperity isn't to be understood purely as success or wealth but as a state of righteousness seen in paths that will exemplify the perfection of His will. He leads us by His Spirit and His written Word.

Your Reflections

Verse 4a

"Yea, though I walk through the valley of the shadow of death, I will fear no evil for Thou art with me."

- Sheep paths are narrow and dangerous through the mountains to the tablelands, but the sheep follow the shepherd without fear.
- When we feel God's presence, we have peace and assurance that He will never leave us nor forsake us.

Upon my first reading, the emphasis seemed to be on "death." It's natural for us to fear death, or the process of it, but if we believe in God's sovereignty, we'll be assured of eternal life with Him. The assurance is a promise that "though"—while, even if—I must go into the valley, the Shepherd will be there. The next day the emphasis was on "through." There was hope for passage *beyond* the Valley of the Shadow of depression and dark, frightening days. I did fear evil, but my Shepherd steadied me and set me free from the bondage of fear which plagued my mind for months, keeping me from fellowship with other believers or going anywhere with my family.

The next emphasis on "I will fear no evil" or "I will not fear" is really not an effort of my will but the manifestation of an obedient mind, body, and spirit *not* to fear. Spiritual warfare is real! One must apply the whole spiritual armor defined in Ephesians 6—especially the helmet of salvation which is full head- and-heart knowledge that one is saved. To go into spiritual warfare each day without this "helmet" is to invite mental attacks. I praise You, Lord, for this revelation.

"Thou art *with* me." Again from Matthew Henry's commentary, "Having had such experience of God's goodness to me all my days, therefore [he] shall still be my strong tower, and shall assure me that he who has led me, and fed me, all my life long, will not leave me at last."

Jesus, You have assured me that You have been with me my whole life and have not—and never will— leave me but walk *with* me even through the valley of the shadow of death.

Your Reflections

Verse 4b

"Thy rod and thy staff,
they comfort me"

- Sheep are helpless and have no ability to defend themselves.
- The shepherd carries a club to protect the sheep from wild predators.
- His staff is used to retrieve sheep from a dangerous ledge – also as a discipline tool.
- God's power realized assures us even as we are helpless.
- God's discipline also helps us to grow and understand His will and power.

The "staff" of the psalm is our tactile connection to the Shepherd until that day when we rest in His arms. His rod is the power in the Name of Jesus as I am in and of myself helpless and a sinner. The staff is the reality of the cross and my personal relationship with Jesus. The vertical relationship of my life—always extending His everlasting arms, always saving to the uttermost.

Donna Riggs

Your Reflections

Verse 5a

"You prepare a table before me in
the presence of my enemies."

- The shepherd has to clear grazing land of
  poisonous and sharp, thorny plants before the sheep can graze safely and also
  see that it is clear of predators who would
  harm the sheep.

- God assures us of the protection of His
  strength and if we accept and obey His
  preparations we will not be harmed. (See
  my personalized version of Psalm 27 in
  Afterthoughts.)

During a past Sunday's communion, I
had a feeling of love and contentment as I
prayed and meditated on Christ's sacrifice
of His body and blood for me. And how in

the midst of my fears or anxieties, i.e. "my enemies," the Lord's table assures me and exhorts me to "remember" and be aware of the power in His death over Satan, sin, and sickness.

It recently occurred to me that the actual removal of my enemies is in the "pastureland" where He leads and feeds me. *He leads me into dangerous territories knowing that He has already provided for my safety.* Jesus Himself was led by the Spirit into the wilderness where he was tempted by Satan at a vulnerable time, after fasting for 40 days. But He did not succumb to the shortcuts His archenemy offered. He answered him with the truth of the Word of God, against which the tempter had no recourse

Sometimes enemies can give one a perverse sense of normalcy. My mother was divorced when I was seven. She had to work and so, doing what she thought was best, she sent me to a boarding school—not a fancy Miss So-and-So's Country Day School, but a place for other children from broken homes, many of whom had special educational needs. This school was run by a very strict headmistress. The girls had one supervisor; the boys had another. They were *not* mother figures by any stretch of the imagination. They were more like, on a good day, benevolent dictators. On the other 300+ days of the year, just dictators.

I lived there for four years except for holidays and a few weeks in the summers. Frankly, I don't remember any of those home visits. But I do remember that for four years every time I had to return to the school—every time I watched my grandfather and my mother drive away, up the oval gravel driveway and out of sight—I stood at the front door sobbing inconsolably until I could hardly breathe. The heaving gasps continued far into the night. The next morning the bullying by my one roommate would begin again. *Life was back to normal.*

Recently a tornado touched down near my home. A huge tree fell across the road and snapped the telephone pole near it in half. Live wires were entangled in the limbs of the tree and the tree people, realizing they were in danger, had to stop using their chain saws and wait for the electric company before they could do any further work on the tree. *We* have to wait and trust God's timing for His provisions and purposes for us. *He* is the faithful Promise Keeper!

Your Reflections

Verse 5b

"You anoint my head with oil;
my cup overflows"

- Sheep need to have soothing oil rubbed into scratches or wounds to help them heal and to keep parasites away.
- Sheep enjoy one-on-one personal care by the shepherd.
- God deals with us personally – He knows our names and ministers to us "right where it hurts".

My Shepherd has tended to my hurts. Someone once said, "How can you say you love me if you don't know what hurts me?" Jesus knows, loves, and delivers me from anxiety and the bondage of fear. This realization, so happily and joyfully received, is indeed an overflowing cup! He has made me feel so loved . . . and loveable. I am worthy of this joy because my Shepherd has cared for and about me.

Your Reflections

Verse 6a

"Surely goodness and mercy shall follow me all the days of my life"

- We can have confidence in the assurance that God knows us individually and will not give up on us.
- He will pursue us with His mercy and goodness – never leave us or forsake us.
- Believing that every day is a day that the Lord has made will allow us to be glad and grateful whatever may come our way.

I praise God today for all the new beginnings He has brought to my life. In the beginning God created beginnings! I pray to greet each new day with praise and thanksgiving and rejoicing. "Surely" is based on my Shepherd's faithfulness and His inability to fail! New mercies will be available to me every day that dawns because He knows I will need them.

Donna Riggs

Your Reflections

Verse 6b

"And I will dwell in the house of the
Lord forever"

- Knowing the God of this psalm assures us
  of a life with Him when our earthly life
  is over.

"No more night.

No more pain.

No more tears;

never crying again.

And praises to the great I AM,

we will live in the light of the Risen Lamb!"

Glory! Amen!

No More Night lyrics © Royalty Network,
Songtrust Ave, Warner Chappell Music, Inc.
Songwriter: Walter S. Harrah

Your Reflections

Afterthoughts

Getting to Know Jesus, Our Shepherd

Genesis 1:1 – In the beginning God created the heavens and the earth.

John 1:1-5 – In the beginning was the Word, *[Greek: Before there was any beginning, the Word had been]* and the Word was with God, and the Word was God. He was in the beginning with God. All things were made through Him, and without Him nothing was made that has been made. In Him was life, and the life was the light of men. And the light shines in the darkness, but the darkness does not comprehend it.

Matthew 1:20-21 – An angel of the Lord appeared to him in a dream, saying, "Joseph, son of David, do not be afraid to take to you Mary your wife, for that which is conceived in her is of the Holy Spirit. And she will bring forth a Son, and you shall call His name Jesus for He will save His people from their sins." [Hebrew: *Yeshua* means *the LORD saves.*]

John 1:10-14 – He was in the world, and the world was made through Him, and the world did not know Him. He came to His own, and His own did not receive Him. But as many as received Him, to them He gave the right to become children of God, to those who believe in His name: who were born, not of blood, nor of the will of the flesh, nor of the will of man, but of God. And the Word became flesh and dwelt among us, and we beheld His glory, the glory as of the only begotten of the Father, full of grace and truth.

John 1:16 (NIV) – From the fullness of His grace we have all received one blessing after another.

Hebrews 1:1-3 – God, who at various times and in various ways spoke in time past to the fathers by the prophets, has in these last days spoken to us by His Son, whom He has appointed heir of all things, through whom also He made the worlds; who being the brightness of His glory and the express image of His person, and upholding all things by the word of His power, when He had by Himself provided purification for our sins, sat down at the right hand of the Majesty on high.

[A simplified explanation: God is creative thought. Jesus is the expression of that thought—the Word. The Holy Spirit is inspiration and memory within us of that Word.]

The sun and its radiance are one and the same. The Son is the radiance of God's glory—not a reflection like the moon.

A person and his personality are one and the same. Jesus is the exact representation of God's being.

Word Study:
from Charles Spurgeon's
Morning and Evening;
Morning January 27

"From the *fullness* of His grace we have all received one blessing after another" (John 1:16, KJV).

These words tell us that there is a fullness in Christ. [*Greek: plēroma – a fullness that stays full, is never depleted*]

There is a fullness of essential Deity, for "in him dwelleth all the fulness of the Godhead." There is a fulness of perfect manhood, for in him, bodily, that Godhead was revealed (see Colossians 2:9, KJV).

There is a fullness of atoning blood, for "the blood of Jesus Christ, his Son, cleanseth us from all sin" (1 John 1:7c, KJV).

There is a fullness of justifying righteousness in his life, for "there is therefore now no condemnation to them that are in Christ Jesus." (Romans 8:1, KJV)

There is a fullness of sufficiency in intercession, for "He is able to save to the uttermost them that come unto God by him;

seeing he ever liveth to make intercession for them" (Hebrews 7:25, KJV).

There is a fullness of victory in his death, for through death he destroyed him that had the power of death, that is the devil (Hebrews 2:14).

There is a fullness of power in his resurrection from the dead, for by it "we are begotten again unto a living hope" (1 Peter 1:3) and "Jesus said to her (Martha), 'I am the resurrection and the life. He who believes in Me, though he may die, he shall live'" (John 11:25).

There is a fullness of triumph in His ascension, for "when he ascended up on high, he led captivity captive, and gave gifts to men" (Ephesians 4:8). The gifts spoken of are explained in Psalm 68 as quoted by Paul. It says, "received gifts for men" that is, "thou hast received gifts" to distribute among men. The impartation of the gifts of the Spirit depended on Christ's ascension (See 1 Corinthians 12:4-11).

There is a fullness of blessings of grace to pardon, of grace to regenerate, of grace to sanctify, of grace to preserve, and of grace to perfect.

There is a fullness of comfort in affliction, of guidance in prosperity.

There is a fullness of the totality of God with all his power and every divine attribute, "for God was pleased to have all His fullness to dwell in Him (Jesus) (see Colossians 1:19).

Psalm 27
(AMP version [personalized for me])

[1] (You, Lord, are) my Light and my Salvation—whom shall I fear *or* dread? (You are) the Refuge *and* Stronghold of my life—of whom shall I be afraid?

[2] When the wicked, even my enemies and my foes (health issues, pain, anxieties, catastrophic imaginations), came upon me to eat up my flesh (to weaken and discourage me), they stumbled and fell.

[3] Though a host encamp against me, my heart shall not fear; though spiritual warfare arise against me, [even then] in (Your strength and power) will I be confident.

[4] One thing have I asked of my Lord, that will I seek, inquire for, *and* [insistently] require: that I may dwell in His house [in His presence] all the days of my life, to behold *and* gaze upon the beauty [the sweet attractiveness and the delightful loveliness] of the Lord and to meditate, consider, *and* inquire in His temple.

[5] For in the day of trouble He will hide me in His shelter (I will not be violated); in the secret place of His tent will He hide me

(I will be nurtured); He will set me high upon a rock.

6 And now shall my head be lifted up above my enemies round about me; in (Your) tent I will offer sacrifices *and* shouting of joy; I will sing, yes, I will sing praises to (You, Lord. I will have a purpose and a testimony – 1 Peter 2:9.)

7 Hear, O Lord, when I cry aloud; have mercy *and* be gracious to me and answer me!

8 You have said, "Seek My face [inquire for and require My presence as your vital necessity]." My heart says to You, "Your face [Your presence]," Lord, will I seek, inquire for, *and* require [of necessity and on the authority of Your Word]. (I will have faith that You will make Your face to shine upon me and be gracious unto me – Numbers 6:24-26.)

9 Hide not Your face from me; turn not Your servant away in anger, You Who have been my help! Cast me not off, neither forsake me, O God of my salvation! (You did not cause Your Son to die for my salvation just to forsake me!)

10 Although my father and my mother have forsaken me, yet (You) Lord, will take me up [*adopt me as (Your) child*]. (Halleluia! I am not abandoned. I am not a foster child who will age out. I am an adopted child of the King forever!)

11 Teach me Your way, O Lord, and lead me

in a plain and even path because of my enemies [those who lie in wait for me].

¹² Give me not up to the will of my adversaries, for false witnesses have risen up against me; they breathe out cruelty *and* violence. (The spiritual warfare is real and the enemy is relentless in his efforts to kill, steal and destroy.)

¹³(But You, Jesus, have come to give abundant life.) I would have fainted unless I had believed that I would see (Your) goodness in the land of the living!

¹⁴ Wait *and* hope for *and* expect the goodness of the Lord; be brave *and* of good courage and let your heart be *determined and* enduring. Yes, (I will) wait for *and* hope for *and* expect: (You, Lord, to be my Light and my Salvation. You are the Refuge and Stronghold of my life.)

A Last Thought

I wanted to add this to my comments about verse 4, "Though I walk through the valley of the shadow of death, I will fear no evil, for You are with me . . ." but it didn't fit there. So I mention it now.

My husband had been ill for quite a while. His last hospitalization was due to a fall he had while trying to reach for his rollator by himself without calling for help. In the ER I was told he had suffered two comminuted fractures of his pelvis—some jagged shards were pressing into the bladder wall. He also suffered one broken collar bone and the other dislocated. They said it would take at least six weeks for him to be able to put weight on his lower body. He would be admitted to the hospital and then eventually moved to rehab.

Every time he had to be moved in his bed or to a gurney to be taken for more CT scans, the pain he was already experiencing became excruciating. A nurse said to me, "If someone has a broken leg or arm it can be isolated, but with injuries like your husband's it's not possible. Every move will affect his pelvis and collar bones." At some

point, around the eighth day of his hospitalization, his doctor came in to talk with
me. He told me my husband's injuries had
so traumatized his body already weakened
by end stage liver disease from hereditary
hemochromatosis and Parkinson's that his
blood cells were breaking apart, his liver
was ceasing to work at all. We were no lon-
ger waiting for rehab; we should prepare
for hospice. I asked how long they expected
him to live. He answered, "We can't really
know. Could be hours or days. It all depends
on how strong his heart is."

He was transported to a hospice facility
where he lived for four more days with only
minimal comfort care. On the third day, I ar-
rived at 10:30 a.m. to find him all tangled up
in his hospital gown trying to get out of it. I
joked with him and said, "Honey, I just got
here. Let me get my jacket off and I'll get an
aide to help get you out of that and into something more comfortable."

The aide and I carefully changed him
into a favorite t-shirt he had from a missions
weekend at church. It read, "Welcome the
Stranger." That change settled him down
and after letting him relax for a few min-
utes, I asked him if he could talk with me. He
turned his head from looking at the ceiling to
look at me beside his bed. I don't know why,
but I asked him, "Do you know who I am?"

"Yes," was the rather perturbed answer.

"Can you tell me my name?"

At this point, he turned quickly to lying
on his back. It was about 10:45. From that

moment, he never moved a muscle, never responded to any stimulus—even pain. After a momentary concern, *I realized that I had witnessed the moment when his spirit left his body.* He was meeting his Shepherd in the valley of the shadow of death, and I was trying to get him to talk to me! His strong, kind, loving heart kept his body alive for another twenty-two hours until he breathed his last on the next afternoon.

I believe it was God's gift to me to be able to see that wonderful moment. It was not dramatic. If I hadn't been trying to get him to talk with me, I would have missed it. But I was blessed to witness it and to be able to remember it instead of the pain of the past weeks as I had to stand by after 52 years of marriage, a helpless helpmate unable to do anything for my husband in his most critical hours. It also gave me a preview into my own future homegoing as I leave this world to be led by my Shepherd through that valley. "Having had such experience of God's goodness to me all my days, therefore [he] shall still be my strong tower, and shall assure me that he who has led me, and fed me, all my life long, will not leave me at last."

Jesus, You have assured me that You have been with me my whole life and have not— and never will—leave me but walk with me even through the valley of the shadow of death.

Introduction to
The Mountainside

Some time after I went through Dr. Allen's writings on Psalm 23 in his book, *God's Psychiatry*, I also journaled my way through his chapter on the Beatitudes. Matthew 5 through 7 are referred to as the Sermon on the Mount. It begins this way in Matthew's gospel: "Now when He saw the crowds, He went up on a mountainside and sat down. His disciples came to Him, and He began to teach them saying . . ." (Matthew 5:1). And the Beatitudes follow.

On the mountainside we see the incarnate Shepherd of David's psalm. David's Shepherd was his faithful, unchanging, caring Protector God whom he had learned about and believed in from his youth. Approximately 1,000 years later, we see Jesus, often referred to as the Son of David, on the mountainside explaining the personal relationship that can be enjoyed in the Kingdom of God. Being defined as "blessed" relates to having received some of the character of God's Christ. Jesus' teaching on the mountainside is for seekers of righteousness—believers—and not for the unregenerate sinner who prefers to love the darkness (see John 3:19).

God's Psychiatry, Charles L. Allen, ©1953 by Fleming H. Revell a division of Baker Book House Company, P.O. Box 6287, Grand Rapids, Michigan 49516-6287

God's Psychiatry Notes

The bullet points after each of the Beatitudes of Matthew 5:3-12 are from Dr. Allen's commentary. As in his teaching on Psalm 23, they are intended to help the reader learn a new pattern of thinking about God and one's relationship to Him. Dr. Allen's points are followed by my reflections. And finally, space is left for you to write Your Reflections. I pray you will be blessed to know the Shepherd of The Pastureland in a very different way as Jesus on The Mountainside equips us to live obediently to the guidance of His Holy Spirit.

The Beatitudes

Matthew 5:3-10

Verse 3

"Blessed are the poor in spirit, for theirs is the kingdom of heaven."

- The poverty which is a key to God's Kingdom is the realization that, though we possess all things, without God all our things are nothing we sometimes interpret the word "blessed" to mean happy, but really it means a oneness with God. The "poor in spirit" have so emptied themselves of themselves – the pride of their accomplishments, the selfishness of their desires – that the Spirit of God has come into their emptiness.

- Notice that Jesus uses the verb "is." His Kingdom is an immediate possession. It is not a place. It is an experience. It is not bounded by geographical lines. It is bounded only by our capacity to receive it.

Spiritual beggars know their need. One who feels no need will receive nothing. Our need includes repenting of spiritual independence—a belief that we are not in constant dependence on all of God's life support systems—a belief that there is such a thing as self-reliance. Jesus had washed His disciples' feet after they broke bread together at the Last Supper, then He taught them many things they would need to remember after He departed from them. Among those was His reminder that "apart from Me you can do nothing" (John 15:5). We need to remember that and know that any time we step out of the shadow of the Cross of Christ, we are exposed to separation from the God Who can only associate with us in the holiness of that shadow. When we come to that realization, Jesus says we have experienced Kingdom blessings.

Thank God that Satan could not succeed in persuading Jesus to have *even one* independent thought! (see Matthew 4:1-11) Jesus only, always did the will of His Father!

Your Reflections

Verse 4

"Blessed are those who mourn, for
they will be comforted."

- Socrates described a man's conscience as
  the wife from whom there is no divorce ...
  but we can stifle it until its voice is com-
  pletely stilled. Ephesians 4:19 tells us of
  certain people who were "past feeling".

- The second Beatitude tells us we should
  be so grieved over our moral and spiritual shortcomings that we cannot rest until we have found God, and our souls are
  satisfied. Those who care to the point of a
  broken spirit and a contrite heart, care to
  a deep repentance.

- Today we want God's blessings without
  the pain of God's purging. But we must
  remember that Christ came to make men
  good rather than merely to make men
  feel good.

To receive God's comfort, we must mourn and be repentant of our sin and the sin of the world. In the process, we become confessors of our own sin and intercessors for those who "know not what they do." Zechariah 12:10 prophesied to the post-exilic Jews that they would grieve bitterly when they look on the One whom they pierced and mourn for Him. When we come to face and experience deep, personal heart-sorrow for our egregious and even "stupid" sins, for which Jesus paid the price, we mourn for our sin to have been the cause of the nails driven through His healing hands and feet that brought us Good News and the mocking crown of thorns to have been painfully pressed into His brow.

> "When I survey the wondrous cross on which the Prince of glory died,
>
> My richest gain I count but loss, and pour contempt on all my pride."

We mourn "in exile," knowing we are not realizing our full spiritual potential. We grieve over the sense of being unfulfilled, incomplete, and especially knowing how our life has not glorified the Lord—how we must be a disappointment to Him. The weight of sin is not felt by those who identify with this world and the gods of it as do those who are born again in Jesus. Jesus cannot be just one among many. He must be all in all. The self-sufficient do not accept that they are sinners, but the greatest sin is pride of self-sufficiency. If I can carry my own burdens, I don't need a Burden Bearer. I am not poor in spirit and do not see any reason to mourn for what others may call sin.

But thankfully, Isaiah brings God's Word of comfort. He wants to comfort those who mourn. In Luke 4, Jesus had returned to Nazareth after the devil tempted Him and went to the synagogue on the Sabbath. There He read from Isaiah 61, identifying Himself as the One spoken of by the prophet: "The Spirit of the Sovereign Lord is on me, because the Lord has anointed me to preach good news to the poor . . . to comfort all who mourn . . ." Through the prophet God gave an earlier assurance of this:"I will not accuse forever, nor will I always be angry, for then the spirit of man would grow faint before me . . . . I have seen his ways, but I will heal him; I will guide him and restore comfort to him" (57:16, 18).

Your Reflections

Verse 5

"Blessed are the meek, for they will inherit the earth."

- The Hebrew word which is translated "meek" really means "to be molded".
- It means to be self-controlled – submissive to the divine plan of God – to accept God's way and live according to His law. For the farmer, it means planting when he should plant. It means submission to God's laws.

Poverty of spirit and mourning for sin lead to meekness or humbly surrendering control of our lives to God. Being yielded, disciplined, and acknowledging His total authority, we accept the truth that apart from Him we can do nothing (see John 15:5) and that all of our help "is in the name [I am] of the Lord" (Psalm 124:8). But meekness does not equal weakness. It has been said that meekness is strength under control. It is the ability to choose to submit one's strength to the Lordship of Jesus. According to a footnote in the *NIV Study Bible*, the meek are "those who humbly acknowledge their dependence on the goodness and grace of God and betray no arrogance toward their fellowman."

Jesus' chosen one to lead His church wrote in his first epistle that we are to follow Christ's example: "He committed no sin and no deceit was found in His mouth. When they hurled their insults at Him, He did not retaliate; when He suffered, He made no threats. Instead, He entrusted Himself to Him who judges justly" (1 Peter 2:22-23). The meek, just like the farmer, submit to God's plan and His timing. Psalm 37:10-11 assures us that, "A little while and the wicked will be no more; though you look for them, they will not be found. But the meek will inherit the land and enjoy great peace." Compare this with Proverbs 11:29 which promises that "he who brings trouble on his family will inherit only the wind."

Your Reflections

Verse 6

"Blessed are those who hunger
and thirst for righteousness,
for they will be filled."

- [Imagination] means to create in our thinking what we want created in our living. Jesus tells us that before we can possess God and the things of God we must first make God the center of our imagination. "Thou shalt love the Lord thy God with all thy heart, and with all thy soul, and with all thy mind" (Matthew 22:37).

- Some have needs that human resources do not supply. They come to church feeling that need, hungering and thirsting for God, and it is they who find Him. You never find God until He becomes your deepest desire....being identified whole-heartedly with God.

- "Thirst" is a strong word, a driving word.

And when the human soul thirsts for God, Jesus says he will be filled with God.

"As the deer panteth for the water, so my soul longeth after Thee. You alone are my heart's desire and I long to worship Thee." This song written in 1984 by Martin Nystrom based on Psalm 42 has always blessed me. But as I sing the lovely melody of the first phrase, I imagine the animal racing through the forest in desperate need of water. His nostrils flare, his mouth is open showing his dry tongue, and he shakes his head with each breath that parches his throat. If he does not find water very soon, he will die of thirst. Is that how my soul longs to worship the living God? Is He my heart's desire? Elisa Morgan writing a devotional for *Our Daily Bread*, asks it in a slightly different way: "Does my heart growl in desire for Him the way my stomach did over the idea of a donut?"

I have often felt a deep hungering need to hear from God. And as the psalmist asks, "My soul thirsts for God, for the living God. When can I go and meet with God?" Even if we know Jesus as our Savior and Lord, it is still possible to have times of spiritual dryness, which can lead us to look for other answers. But even if we do wrong, 1 John 1:9 assures us that we are still in right standing with God because of Jesus' righteousness: "If we confess our sins, he is faithful and just and will forgive us our sins and purify us from all unrighteousness."

When the enemy tries to tell me who I'm not, I can agree that my righteousness is as filthy rags (see Isaiah 64:6) and declare that my human virtue is covered by the perfect purity, justice, and integrity of Jesus! He said in John 6:35, "I am the bread of life. Whoever comes to me will never go hungry, and whoever believes in me will never be thirsty." He says we will be filled: "He satisfies my mouth with *good* things" (Psalm 103:5).

Many unfortunately do not look for that thirst-quenching water in the right places but continue to dig in the sand of false promises that will never slake their God-designed thirst for the living water of the living God.

Your Reflections

Verse 7

"Blessed are the merciful, for they will
be shown mercy."

- Of the eight Beatitudes, this one is the
  most appealing, the most important, and
  the most difficult. All of us have sinned
  and come short of God's glory. (Romans
  3:23) The only prayer we can pray is,
  "God, be merciful to me a sinner" (Luke
  18:13).

- However, the key to God's mercy toward
  ourselves is the mercy we have toward
  others. "If ye forgive not men their trespasses, neither will your Father forgive
  your trespasses" (Matthew 6:15).

- Mercy requires not only a right spirit on our part against a person who has
  wronged us...but we must do even more....
  Mercy requires that we sow good seed in
  our enemy's field, even though it means

that part of our own field will be left bare. It is not easy. It is the hardest possible action, but it is our key to God's Kingdom.

- The way of the world was an eye for an eye and a tooth for a tooth. Jesus came offering men a higher way and a better life, but [when] men stood back to mock and to laugh and to crucify He uttered the word, "Forgive."

And when He did, His divine request for forgiveness extended much further than to those in His immediate world. It extended to each and all who would receive His offer of salvation by means of His death and resurrection. He continues once and for all to be one Son for all.

When we are wronged or hurt, the resentment we might feel can easily become hate. We can make the decision to fan the fires of bitterness. Or we can remember that *we* don't and can't merit God's mercy, but in receiving it we can become more merciful. We can sow good seed and show kindness toward the one who hurt us instead of becoming an "oil spill" of resentment that affects everyone who must live with us in that bitterness that defiles many (see Hebrews 12:15).

Your Reflections

Verse 8

"Blessed are the pure in heart,
for they will see God."

- A person sees God through the eyes of the heart; Jesus said: "He that hath seen me hath seen the Father." (John 14:9) Certainly not every person who saw Him with his physical eyes saw God. Mere physical sight of Him revealed only a man....Really to see God in Christ one must experience Him in the heart.

- "Eye hath not seen, nor ear heard, neither have entered into the heart of man, the things which God hath prepared for them that love Him" (1 Corinthians 2:9). There we have pointed out three kinds of sight. [There is] the sight of the natural eye . . . hearing or reading something to the point of understanding. But there is still a third sight, as when a truth has "entered into the heart of man."

- How we see God depends on the condition of our hearts.

What does it mean to be pure in heart? Psalm 24:4-5 answers the question for us: "He who has clean hands and a pure heart, who has not lifted up his soul to an idol, nor sworn deceitfully. He shall receive blessing from the Lord." An unpure heart is compromising and has divided, fleshly desires. Whatever standards we use to recognize a person as pure by looking at their appearance, God's standard is to look at the heart (see 1 Samuel 16:7). A pure heart is undivided in total devotion to God. If our heart is pure, our desire is to seek for God, to know Him and please Him: "And you will seek Me and find Me when you search for me with all your heart" (Jeremiah 29:13).

Our motives for the choices we make come from our deceitful hearts and, though we wouldn't realize it, they are mostly made on the basis of the gain or loss we will realize. If we have nothing to lose, it is easy enough to stand "courageously" against slavery, for instance. But if we reap benefit from it, we would be convinced that there is nothing wrong with it. Because of the original sin of doubting, disobeying, or misunderstanding God's command not to eat from the tree of the knowledge of good and evil, humankind has trusted their own evaluation of things that only our omniscient God can determine. And so we lift up our souls to idols whose purpose it is to make us unable to see God.

Your Reflections

Verse 9

"Blessed are the peacemakers, for they
will be called children of God."

- Above all things, peace is the desire of my
  heart and yours. We want peace in our
  world – we want peace inside ourselves.

- The angel climaxed the announcement
  of the birth of our Lord with the words,
  "Glory to God in the highest, and on earth
  peace, good will toward men." (Luke
  2:14) Peace was Jesus' mission. "Peace
  I leave with you, my peace I give unto
  you." (John14:27) When we think of the
  Kingdom of God we think of a kingdom
  of peace, where all strife has ceased.

- The mere absence of strife is not peace
  . . . Peace is a positive force. You may
  clear some plot of land of every noxious
  weed, but that will not make it a garden
  . . . Swords must become plowshares
  and the spears pruning hooks . . . Peace
  is something to be made: thus we must

be peacemakers if we are to enter the Kingdom of God.

When we become peace*makers*, we reflect the likeness of Christ. Just a few verses after this, Jesus said,

> "You are the light of the world. A city on a hill cannot be hidden. Nor do they light a lamp and put it under a basket, but on a lampstand, and it gives light to all who are in the house. Let your light so shine before men that they may see your good works and glorify your Father in heaven" (Matthew 5:14-16).

He called us children of our Father God!

Most in this world would rather be powermakers than peacemakers. As in the Garden of Eden, the temptation is always there to be like God in power, not as His recognizable child. I remember being blessed back in the day when I heard young Amy Grant's song, "My Father's Eyes." "When people look inside my life, I want to hear them say, 'She's got her Father's Eyes, her Father's Eyes. Eyes that find the good in things when good is not around. Eyes that find the source of help when help just can't be found. Eyes full of compassion seeing every pain knowing what you're going through and feeling it the same.'" These are the qualities of a peacemaker who unmistakably resembles their Father.

To be that kind of peacemaker, one must first receive the shalom that Christ offered "by making peace through His blood shed on the cross" (Colossians 1:29). Peacemaking requires sacrifice and hard work—both travailing in prayer and actually doing things that bring peace. The Apostle Paul exhorted the newly-planted Ephesian church to "*make every effort* to keep the unity of the Spirit through the bond of peace" (Ephesians 4:3, emphasis added). I read somewhere that the word "bond" could have the sense of tying a cord around all different shapes and sizes of twigs and branches. Others may think of this as trying to avoid sibling rivalry or "nailing Jell-o to a tree." But it's the necessary work required to make peace and keep the unity of the Spirit. To quote a former pastor of mine, "It's not easy. But it's Kingdom!"

Your Reflections

Verse 10

"Blessed are those who are persecuted because of righteousness, for theirs is the kingdom of heaven."

- Jesus never promised ease to those who follow Him. Never did he put a carpet on the racetrack or a bed of roses on the battlefield. He talked about self-denial, about crosses – blood-spattered, death-dealing crosses. To enter the Kingdom of God [heaven] may mean decisions that are hard, consecration that leads to persecution. But it can be no other way.

- No person ever really lives until he has found something worth dying for. You can never really possess the Kingdom of God until the cause of God becomes more important than your own life.

- To be poor in spirit means to give up our pride; to mourn means to be penitent to the point of surrendering our sins; meekness means that we must surrender our very selves to the plans and purposes of God; our hunger for God means turning away from our ambitions for all things else; to be merciful means to pay good for the evil we have received; for purity we must give up things impure; to make peace is wholly to choose God. Those are the seven ingredients of righteousness. They must be bought at a price. Blessed are those who pay the price, "for theirs is the kingdom of God."

Jesus wants us to recognize the full value of the Kingdom. It is worth suffering persecution, fighting for, dying for. There is a difference between what some call stupid suffering and redemptive suffering. The former is caused by the consequences of our bad life choices. The latter is because of our association with Christ. These are some of the things Jesus said which fit into that category: "All men will hate you because of me, but he who stands firm to the end will be saved" (Matthew 19:22); "If the world hates you, keep in mind that it hated me first" (John 15:18). And the Apostle Paul encouraged us with this thought from 2 Timothy 2:12, "If we endure, we will also reign with Him" in His Kingdom.

John the Baptist had doubts about his suffering when he was imprisoned for confronting Herod and his adultery. John had unmet expectations. *Why are the righteous persecuted for challenging what is wicked and standing up for what is right?* He sent two of his disciples to Jesus to seek an answer from Him (Matthew 11:3), "Are you the one who was to come, or should we expect someone else?" After he had identified and baptized Jesus, heard the voice of God and seen the Holy Spirit descending like a dove and lighting on Him, John still doubted. Jesus did not chastise John for doubting but sent his disciples back to assure him that everything was going as planned and to give him this benediction: "Blessed is the man who is not offended on account of me" (11:6). Like John, most of us at one time or another have asked the wrong question by focusing on the immediate, temporal, and personal while Jesus was working in the realm of the Kingdom eternal.

Persecution is the inevitable result of our light challenging those who prefer the darkness. John 3:19 is clear: "This is the verdict: Light has come into the world, but men loved the darkness instead of the light because their deeds were evil." While the righteous become disciplined to live in the authority of God's Kingdom, the world is enraged by it, will not tolerate it, and will attempt to destroy it by any means necessary. Jesus was and is our example: "He did not retaliate; when He suffered, He made no threats. Instead, He entrusted Himself to Him who judges justly" (1 Peter 2:22-23). God will make the final judgment for those who are persecuted for righteousness' sake, and their efforts will be richly rewarded. "For this light momentary affliction is preparing us for an eternal weight of glory beyond all comparison, as we look not to the things that are seen but to the things that are unseen. For the things that are seen are transient, but the things that are unseen are eternal" (2 Corinthians 4:17).

Your Reflections on The Beatitudes